# THE WAY WE WERE

## ALL AGES

*The Way We Were* has power to put you back to where you belong. Just receive it.

### By Lex Francois

Copyright © 2012 by Lex Francois

*The Way We Were!*
by Lex Francois

Printed in the United States of America

ISBN 9781622307180

All rights reserved solely by the author. The author guarantees all contents are original and do not infringe upon the legal rights of any other person or work. No part of this book may be reproduced in any form without the permission of the author. The views expressed in this book are not necessarily those of the publisher.

Unless otherwise indicated, Bible quotations are taken from the King James version. Copyright © 1989 by World Publishing, Nashville, TN.

www.xulonpress.com

# CONTENTS

Chapter 1:  Where We Are Today ........9
Chapter 2:  My Upbrining ....................21
Chapter 3:  Having Your Own Way .....29
Chapter 4:  Who Am I? .........................39
Chapter 5:  Be An Example .................50
Chapter 6:  Sitting Idly By ...................58
Chapter 7:  The Church .......................63
Chapter 8:  What God Wants ...............77
Chapter 9:  How Can We Return?........84
Chapter 10: Victory Is Around
            The Corner .......................91

# **DEDICATION**

This book is lovingly dedicated to the memory of my grandmother, Iris Patrick. She taught me to love God and diligently live for Him.

# INTRODUCTION

This is about encouraging believers in Christ who are sometimes discouraged by what they see taking place in the church. This book will give you courage to stand and declare the righteousness of the Lord. This book will encourage you to be bold and effect change in order to come back to the place you were, no matter the challenges you may face.

The church is under attack on every side, but we will not fail, we will not surrender, we will not give in. Matthew 16:18 says, "And I say also unto thee, that thou art Peter, and upon this rock I will build my church; and the gates of hell shall not prevail against it."

My friend, be encouraged that the church shall not be defeated. You may go through a rough time, persecution after persecution. After reading this book, you will realize that you need to act and act quickly to get back to that place where you used to be in the Lord. You will gain the self-confidence to effect change and go forward in the power of Christ.

# CHAPTER 1

# Where We Are Today

Today's developments and technological advancement in the world bring us into a place where **our passions are flared and our hearts and affections are set on things that we've become so attached to that we pay no attention to the really important stuff in life.** However, we all have varying interests, and what may be important to you may not be the same for others. With such developments, the day is full of activities, and of course it just might be fulfilling to some of us. However, because we have not been careful, we have developed into a self-seeking society.

For example, when you hit the road in your expensive car, give a nod to the neighbor while you drive along the way or sometimes keeping your head forward to avoid making eye contact with him. The rain fell, and the road is wet. You may splash water on that person standing on the side when you pass by in your car, without considering his or her feelings. My friend, I tell you that such actions are inconsiderate and could amount to selfishness.

## SELFISHNESS OF PEOPLE!

To be selfish is to be concerned chiefly with one's own interests or pleasure. My friend, because of the fast pace at which everything moves in the world, you may not pay attention to your neighbor's plight. Perhaps he may not have food to eat or good clothing to wear; he just may not have enough money to go around. Perhaps you recognize and refuse to assist him or her. You understand why I mentioned development and technological advancement in the world; it is because this looks like it has replaced the really good values of selflessness. **Selfishness has crept in over a period of time. Technology and development are good as we make progress as a people, but we should not allow them to take the place of moral and spiritual values.**

My friend, sometimes we focus so much on our own business that we can't see the need of our neighbors. Do you remember those days when what your neighbor had was yours and what you had was your neighbor's? Those days are long gone, and we may never return to them. The Bible says in the last days people will be lovers of themselves, lovers of money, boastful, proud, abusive, disobedient to their parents, ungrateful, unholy, and lovers of pleasure more than lovers of God… (2 Tim. 3:2–9).

Today people don't care about others in the way they once did. **People no longer**

**have time to help each other, to serve one another, to pray for others; they are often too busy trying to get what they want for themselves.** Such ways of life lead to inconsideration. I could go so far as to say wickedness, thoughtlessness, prejudice, selfishness, egocentricity, etc. In fact, we pass people on the streets without extending courtesies or any form of manners that impact positively on their lives. You see, the Word of God is plain, where it says that God will not show mercy on the one who judges people who are less fortunate and instead scorns them; mercy should reign over judgment.

My advice: Do not forget or neglect to show kindness and goodness, to be generous and distribute and contribute to the needs of others as embodiment and proof of a person who did not allow the development of the world to change your perspective of the real values of life. Such sacrifices are pleasing to

God; that is, the sacrifice of giving of oneself to see that others are made happy.

Someone may need food, drink, or shelter, but when he asks some people for assistance, all they do is offer to pray and nothing is given to him to eat. Tell me, what does this demonstrate? Prayer without action is meaningless to the man who is hungry. In the Bible, Jesus not only prayed for the people, but He gave them something to eat as well. Do you remember the five loaves and two fishes in John 6:5–14?

Today there are brothers and sisters who are in need of clothes and don't have food to eat. **What good is there in your saying to them, "God bless you, keep warm and eat well," if you do not give them the necessities to bring about a change in their status?** So if it's prayer alone and there is no action, then that prayer is pointless and self-centered. But someone who prays and demonstrates the love that we confess will reach the heart of the one who is in need. You see, he became selfless to ensure that the need was met. You should show your faith by your actions. Just as a body without the spirit is dead, so too faith without works is dead (James 2:15–26).

There are some people who just talk of helping others and never fulfill their promises. God dislikes people who never honor their vows, for a man is also judged by his word because his word is his vow. **At times we make promises just to impress others, but we will be held accountable for every word that comes out of our mouths.** Never make a promise you cannot keep. If you are unable to assist, just say so. However, you should make every effort to help in the situations of others. Start practicing to lend assistance to others in any small way.

## HAVE COMPASSION!

Proverbs 19:17 says, "He that hath pity upon the poor lendeth unto the Lord; and that which he hath given will he pay him again."

*Where We Are Today*

**God expects us to show mercy and have compassion on those who are less fortunate.** It should be our nature to help someone in need. True believers will love their neighbors as they love themselves.

Today we see individuals in need, and we criticize and judge them. For example, you may be walking down the road and you see a poor, homeless, desolate person. You scorn him or her, looking away or judging. A man may ask you for some money and you say to yourself, He is a big strong man. He could go and work. Or, He wants money to purchase drugs.

My friend, instead of insulting him, ask if he needs something to eat, and show love, care, and support. Perhaps the people who are on the streets could have some kind of burden because of some existing problems in their lives, and there is no one with a shoulder for them to lean on; hence, the reason for their condition. **So please don't add to their burdens; assist them in carrying the**

**burdens. If we show courtesy and just give a smile,** sometimes these simple acts will bring some kind of happiness and relief of pressure to them. You should demonstrate values that may impact positively on their lives. First Corinthians 15:52 says don't be tired of well-doing because your reward is not in vain. You shall be rewarded for doing good deeds and expressing compassion to others.

I had an encounter with a homeless person in Port of Spain, the capital of Trinidad and Tobago. He asked me for money to buy something to eat, so I offered to purchase a burger for him. The man said, "No problem." However, when I bought the burger and handed it to him, he threw it back at me and said, "What can I do with that? I can't do anything with this." I was blown away, but this did not stop me from offering assistance to others in the future. Our character is to do good at all times in spite of the treatment we may experience.

## DISCIPLINE OR DISRESPECT?

It is known that not only do children disrespect each other, but senior folks do also. This has become the order of the world today. **If a young man thinks that you have offended him, both he and his friends may devise a plan to get back at you, or he could try to hurt you** so he can have some form of satisfaction in his heart for what he considers to be payback for disrespect. No wonder the Bible says that "the heart of man is desperately wicked above all things" (Jer. 17:9–10). God does not like such thought of mischief, but these are some of the characteristics displayed by young people who lack good behavior while growing up. It is innate in the human DNA to misbehave; hence, the reason we need to train up a child in the way he should go.

Bring up your children in the admonition and fear of the Lord, according to Ephesians

6:4. My question is, who teaches them such things and who influences their thoughts? You know everything must begin somewhere! You just read that in the opening of this chapter. **Today many people are taken aback because it seems to be a strange thing these days when a young person expresses courtesy and shows a level of manners to an elder.** The norm is to just stare at someone and say nothing when we pass them by in the corridors and roadways.

Most senior folks think that younger people have no manners. Seniors express shock when young people reciprocate their courtesy, more so if the youth manifests manners upon meeting the senior. It is said that parents do not raise children to be respectful anymore. That is why parents have to be an example to their children, because children learn what they see older ones do, which you will read about in the following chapter.

In 2007, one of my neighbors came into the shop where my mom is the proprietor.

The girl was no more than thirteen years old. I heard expletives being exchanged between herself and another young lady. Out of concern, I said to her, "Little girl, you should not behave in such a manner." Do you know what her response was? It was a swift and shocking use of expletives as she said, "Why don't you mind your own business!"

Hearing the expletives, I was so surprised that my mouth hung open for about forty seconds. My thoughts were wild (all over the place), thinking of the utter disrespect from one who should display good manners. Was she disciplined, or was she disrespectful? You can judge for yourself. **Parents, it is your duty to teach your children good values so that when they go into public places, they will be well mannered and disciplined.** Parents, if you display bad manners, generally that's what you will get from your children. What is even more astonishing is the fact that parents are supporting their children in bad behavior; we see this happening all the time.

There's an old saying that goes like this: **"The mango doesn't fall far from the tree"; that is to say, exactly what the parent is, you can expect the child to be the same.** You must guide your children from a disrespectful path onto a path that will command the respect of others as well as their peers.

# CHAPTER 2

# MY UPBRINGING

Today many people do not know how to bring up their children in the right way and in the admonition of the Lord. Because of this, they lose them to many circumstances. Therefore, it is necessary to help in the development of your children, so I share my experience growing up with you so you can gain some valuable principles to teach your children.

I grew up with my grandmother in a little village called Enterprise in the borough of Chaguanas in central Trinidad, West Indies. I lived with her for all my childhood days and part of my adult life. My father and mother did not live together. Statistics show that quite a few children in Trinidad and Tobago grow up with grandparents or within an extended family.

This might be so for a number of reasons, including single parents or difficult economic circumstances that see parents migrating to the United States or Britain, but very few as a result of the parent being too young to take care of the child. **Despite all the situations and problems as a single parent, you don't have to give up your responsibility, as in the case of some people. Show love to your children unconditionally,** and ask God for the inner strength to raise them in godliness. It is very challenging for a single mother to raise a child on her own.

## A GOOD FOUNDATION

My friend, please permit me to share with you some of the experiences I had while growing up with my grandmother. Early in the morning, she would wake me up and say, **"Don't let the sun rise on you."** Then she instructed me to pray, which I did as a child and on through to my adult life. Of course, she was the one who prayed, and I learned from her, but not with the exact words. My grandmother would say to both me and my other cousins, "Always thank God for the day you've entered. Thank Him during the day, and thank Him before you go to bed at night." Often she would read the Bible to me, and she would let me read as well.

It is important to lay the right foundation for your young ones. My friend, when you give your children a foundation of faith in God, they can build a lifetime upon it. "Train up a child in the way he should go: and when he is old, he will not depart from it," says Proverbs 22:6. As a good father or mother, you must do your best to teach your children the laws of God. God holds us responsible for this. Deuteronomy 6:7–8 says, "And thou shalt teach them diligently unto thy children, and shalt talk of them when thou sittest in thine house, and when thou walkest by the way, and when thou liest down, and when thou riseth up."

This tells me that a good foundation early in life is very important for individuals to be set on the right course in life, not only in society, but it will affect their relationship with God. My cousins and I were instructed by Grandma, as she was fondly called, to manifest good manners and courtesy to our elders and those in authority. Those of us who listened to sound doctrine from an early age have reaped the benefits.

Chores were a normal part of growing up. We were required to give assistance in all the house-related work, and the pigs, cows, and goats were also our responsibility. We worked very hard from a young age. If we told our elders that we were unable to do the chores,

*My Upbringing*

we had to be prepared to stay hungry for a day or two. If you don't work, you can't eat! This action on the part of my grandmother was in no way meant to starve you, but to foster ambition in you that you don't become a lazy lad.

You see, my friend, love is a responsibility. My son or daughter, because your mother disciplines you does not mean that she hates you. You know that when someone loves you, they will discipline you. Even God disciplines His loved ones to make them better people. Revelation 3:19 states, "I rebuke and punish all whom I love. Be in earnest, then, and turn from your sins."

Some may say that if you love, you will not discipline a person because it may hurt their feelings or cause them to dislike you for disciplining them for wrongdoing. Discipline, on the contrary, cannot cause any such thing. **Discipline, in the right attitude, will bring about godly fear.** Proverbs 13:24 says, "He that spareth his rod hateth his son: but he that loveth him chasteneth him betimes." A godly foundation must be laid so that children can build upon it and set themselves up for a lifetime of blessings. To neglect your responsibility would be a travesty.

## DON'T SPARE THE ROD

My friend, I was not always a good boy, in a manner of speaking. I was rather mischievous at best and very rude at times, to say the least. One time when I shouted at my mom while she was cautioning me about my bad ways, I received a slap in the face. I learned my lesson almost immediately and never shouted at my elders again. That's the way I was, but I was always going to church with my grandmother. Once I stole a couple of hundred dollars from my granny. When she found out, I was dealt a couple of strokes from the tamarind whip. Only when I became older did I understand why she had to discipline me. **If you leave**

**your children to do wrong, you will not only mislead them, but you may also lead them to think that it's okay to do wrong and that this wrong will go unpunished**. My grandmother disciplined me in love.

Proverbs 3:11–12 says, "My son, despise not the chastening of the Lord; neither be weary of his correction: For whom the Lord loveth he correcteth; even as a father the son in whom he delighteth." (You can also look at Hebrews 12:5.) Often I would run away and go to the pond to bathe, and on my return home, I would be sold out by the white residue on my skin and the redness of my eyes. The tamarind whip would cross my back a few times until I repented of the act of disobedience. Another time I stole someone's toy pedal car, and of course, the whip spoke to me. By now I learned my lesson and really had to practice what I was taught by my grandmom.

Sometimes strangers would pass by and beg lodging for the night. I would be asked by my grandmother to let that person sleep on the bed while I slept on the floor. From time to time, my grandmother and I would travel to Blanchisseuse on the north coast for the summer holidays. While we were sitting on the bus, if there was an old lady standing, my grandmother would instruct me to stand and let the lady sit. Now I would have to stand all the way to Blanchisseuse, through the north coast and the northern range. She might even say, "You young people have no respect for older folks."

I grew into a fine young man. So, my friend, it is awfully important not to spare the rod. This does not mean that you have to abuse your children physically, but it does means you can speak to them sternly and perhaps take measures that will bring about the desired results, without violating their rights. As the Bible says in Proverbs 22:6, "Train up a child in the way he should go: and when he is old, he will not depart from it."

# CHAPTER 3

# HAVING YOUR OWN WAY

## WHAT VALUES DO YOU HAVE?

The youth of today have a different temperament from those of the 1970s and 1980s, as they are generally impatient, rash, rude, and unmannerly, among other things. Statistics show that the degeneration and degradation of a people and society have a lot to do with their moral and spiritual values. **People have become so cold-hearted that there is scarcely any care and love for themselves, let alone for their fellow human beings.** You read earlier where some,

*The Way We Were!*

if not all, of our values have been replaced by arrogance and lack of productivity.

You see, the amount of time we spend on the computer and on electronic games takes away from the time we should be spending with our families in building relationships. I am not against technology, by no means; nonetheless, we should harness it to do well.

You might be driving down the street and you just might get a bad drive from another driver (he cuts you off). Instead of apologizing, the driver might cuss at you and disrespect you. He might have the tendency to become violent and more abusive, while his wife and child are in the car looking on. What an example for children to follow in a time when we are desperately losing our generation.

You see, the reason many people behave this way is that they're not temperate and patient. Then, some people are just acting out their frustration. **Parents, be good examples. Teach your children how to be peaceful in**

**difficult situations and how to manage the emotion of anger.** Parents, do not be afraid to impart good values to your children from a young age. Studies have shown that children between the ages of one to five years old learn faster than at any other time in life. Proper guidance must be given during this period so the children will grow to be well mannered and respectable, intelligent beings.

However, many parents will say their child is just a baby and will outgrow the bad behavior. This quite often is not the case. Instead, we have young people becoming more delinquent and of whose behavior parents are ashamed in the future. You see, it is unwise to leave children to themselves. Parents must provide guidance to them at all times. Even when they reach a legal age, they may still need input from the parents.

I work for a state-owned company. While conducting a safety audit on the contractor's tank wagons, it was discovered that these trucks were defective and unsafe to operate on the roads. One of the owners of a trucking company came to my house and offered me a sum of money to pass his defective trucks. I bluntly refused and informed him that I didn't need his money and he needed to get his trucks roadworthy by doing the necessary repairs.

My integrity would have been questioned, and I would have been obligated to this businessman. Not only that, but I would have been putting the lives of the driver and hundreds of road users at risk by overlooking the severity of the defects and potential danger by allowing these trucks to go on the road with flammable products while being defective. I reported the matter to the relevant authorities.

The Bible warns against the taking of bribes. Exodus 23:8 says, "And thou shalt take no gift: for the gift blindeth the wise, and perverteth the words of the righteous." It is also mentioned in 1 Samuel 8:3, where Samuel's sons were judges and turned away from the path of righteousness. They perverted the course of justice and got involved in other illegal activities. The verse says, "And his sons walked not in his ways, but turned aside after lucre, and took bribes, and perverted judgment."

Today a lot of people—judges, ministers of all kinds, and laymen—take bribes. Your integrity must speak for itself. There is a price to pay for the taking of bribes. It may bring your family name into disrepute for the remainder of your life. Do the right thing. Be bold and strong, and let your integrity stand out.

## THE NAIVE

Teenagers and young adults are shouting and talking down to their parents. Adolescents may test the will of their parents to see how much the parents will tolerate the kind of friends they have, the places they hang out, and the type of activities they're involved in, not forgetting the late nights out.

Then we have the issue of gangs and gang leaders, who may scout your child for recruitment into the gangs. You child might join the gang if he feels rejected by those who should be close to him and feels accepted by those members of the gang who appear to show love and affection. And also, show appreciation for the behavior your youngster displays. Gang leaders only use the young and naive for the sole purposes of the gang's agenda, when the reality is that the gangs don't care about the youngsters.

Because of lack of knowledge and information, people perish. We should allow our children to gain meaningful experiences with proper guidance so they will not be found wanting. Teach your children godly values, and make them knowledgeable so they can make the right choices. Give them an opportunity to have a wealth of knowledge so they will be able to make informed decisions that will affect them for the rest of their lives.

## HAVING NO DISCIPLINE

Young people who do not have a solid foundation from a tender age are more likely to fall prey to gangsters. It is common knowledge that when you are rebellious, you think that you know everything, you are always right, and you have all the answers to life's questions. Because you did not correct your children when they went wrong, they grew up being rebellious. This may lead into difficult problems of which they may not be able to get out off, so please discipline your children.

You know, some young folks just love doing crazy things to embarrass their parents, most times in public places. Children use psychology on parents; they even try burning out parents to cause the parent to give up on discipline.

Why is this so? Because you give them the leeway to do anything they want, and you say stuff like, "He's young; he will come around."

*The Way We Were!*

Parents, stop playing with your children's future! You need to stand your ground as a parent where this is concerned. Continue to express and demonstrate love and affection, but you also must be firm when it comes to correcting and guiding your children. For the Bible says in Proverbs.13:24, "He that spareth his rod hateth his son: but he that loveth him chasteneth him betimes." So you see, true love will desire your children to be placed on the good path of life. Parents, teach values to your children; it will benefit them in the future.

Please do not get me wrong. This does not necessarily mean that you punish them by way of a licking. Correcting and punishing them can also be such as depriving children of certain things they enjoy. Of course you can't deprive your children of their basic rights and privileges; that is, food, shelter, love and affection, and of course protection. You can ground them or tell them no TV for the next four days, etc. You cannot afford not to take control of your children if you want to avoid serious embarrassment and pain in the future. Please remember the admonition of the Bible in Proverbs 13:24: "He that spareth his rod hateth his son: but he that loveth him chasteneth him betimes."

If my grandmother had not corrected me but left me to be wayward and undisciplined, I just might have become a delinquent. Given the environment in which I lived as a teenager, it was very easy to be influenced by the wrong people. My point is this: a determent is necessary to guide a child or a young person in the right direction. My friend, you must direct the course of your child's life.

The early years of guidance will bring a lifetime of joy. When left to themselves, children often make the wrong choices. Whether you like it or not, discipline to children is governed by the state, and the state has failed miserably. The state's measures in this regard have contributed to more delinquency in modern times than in any other period of history. Children know this, and they take advantage of it.

You need to work hard to get discipline and guidance back into your hands so as to fashion godly children in society. As people of God, we have to instill godly fear in the hearts and minds of young people. You cannot afford not to discipline your children if you want them to avoid a lifetime of pain and suffering.

# CHAPTER 4

# WHO AM I?

In this chapter, you will learn how to change your status if you are not a child of the most high to become a son of God!

Who am I? This is a question that many people ask themselves from time to time but seldom have an accurate answer for. In the book of John, chapter 1, we've got some answers for you. *Who am I?* John1:12 says, **"But as many as received him, to them gave he power to become the sons of God, even to them who believe on his name."** In order to know who you are, you must go back to the source; that is, where you came from.

In this chapter, you will learn how to change who you are to become a son of God! **The real children of God can declare that they are God's.** Everyone can say that, but everyone doesn't have the right to do so. Who you are will determine your destiny and what type of relationship you will enjoy with the Lord, be it a close one or one that is far off.

## SIN SEPARATED US

My friend, do not be fooled. All humans are God's creation, but we are not all His children **(1 John 3:2; John 12:48; John 1:12–13).** You see, God created the heavens and the earth, the animals and all living things. We can look at the account in Genesis 1. He created Adam and Eve, the first human couple from which we all came. However, because of Adam's sin, we were all separated from God. Isaiah 59:2 says, "But your iniquities have separated between you and your God, and your sins have hid his face from you, that he will not hear."

My brother and my sister, **sin broke the relationship that we had with our heavenly Father.** That means anything that is filled with sin cannot be in the presence of God. My friend, sin makes you powerless, hopeless, and lonely. It separates you. "You see, at just the right time, when we were still powerless, Christ died for the ungodly" (Rom. 5:6). In Genesis 3:8, we read that God used to walk in the garden in the cool of the day and fellowship with Adam and Eve. This is how close God was with mankind. But all of this came to an end because man sinned against God. However, you are not helpless anymore; someone brought reconciliation back to you. He is the Son of God, named Jesus Christ.

## RECONCILIATION BRINGS US BACK

My friend, **to know and understand who you are, you must get back to God, and to get back to God, you must repent of your sin and believe on God's only provision for**

**sin, His Son Jesus Christ.** He came to bring freedom from sin, which separates you from your God. This wall can be broken only by the blood of the Son of God. Believing and having faith by praying sincerely from the heart can bring reconciliation back to your life.

My friend, 1 John 1:9 says, "If we confess our sins, he is faithful and just to forgive us our sins, and to cleanse us from all unrighteousness." His forgiveness makes you free from the debt that you owe Him. That means you will no longer be judged for sin, and since you are free, this puts you back in direct relationship with God.

My friend, **if you are reading this book and you once had a relationship with the Lord Jesus Christ but that relationship is now broken, then you need to mend it and be reconciled to the Lord.** The same applies to you who do not have a relationship with the Lord. Say this prayer and be reconciled to your Father: "Father, I confess with my mouth that Jesus is Lord, and I believe in my heart that You, God, raised Jesus Christ from the dead. I now by faith invite the Lord Jesus Christ to come into my heart and be the Savior of my life" (see Romans 10:9–11).

Beloved, God has forgiven you. Beloved, do you remember when the prodigal son left his father's house after taking the inheritance that he was entitled to, in Luke 15:11–24? He was separated from his father. The Scriptures say that he joined himself to the people of that country far away and indulged in riotous living; that is, living that was contrary to the life shown to him by his father. The actions of this son drove a wedge between his father and him, causing separation between the two. He wasted all his inheritance on friends and things that were not worth the while.

Just like sin separated us from God, in the same way, this son's actions separated him from his father. Not until he came to his senses—that is to say, not until he realized his condition and that he needed to change and seek forgiveness from his father and actually carry out the act of repenting for his rebellion against his father—was the relationship repaired. In the same way, we need to realize that we must repent of our rebellion against God and actually carry out the act. Therefore, when God forgives us, He removes the wedge that separates us from Him. **And just like with the prodigal son, He reconciles us to Himself, bringing us back into relationship, restored.** This reconciliation brings us who were far off closer to God than we have ever been before.

## THE HOLY SPIRIT COMES INTO YOUR LIFE

Now you are sons and daughters, after repentance and reconciliation, and God fills you with His Spirit, which identifies you as sons and witnesses. John 14:16–17 says, "And I will prayer the Father, and he shall give you another comforter, that he may abide with you forever; even the Spirit of truth, whom the world cannot receive, because it seeth him not, neither knoweth him: but ye know him; for he dwelleth with you; and shall be in you."

My friend, this is true: "If anyone be in Christ, he is a new creation; old things are passed away; behold, all things have become new" (2 Cor. 5:17). So if all things have become new, you (we) have put away old things and embraced the new things.

We are only God's children when the Spirit of God comes and dwells inside of us. You should notice in verse 17 of John 14 where it states "the world cannot receive him," meaning the created human beings who do not know God and who don't have the Spirit of God in them cannot say that they are God's children. Jesus made it clear that they are not His own. Only those who have the Spirit of God in them can say that He is their Father and they are His children.

## I AM A CHILD OF GOD

My friend, now as you are given the power to become a son or daughter of God, you must realize that you are grafted into a royal line. "But ye are a chosen generation, a royal priesthood, an holy nation, a peculiar people; that ye should shew forth the praises of him who hath called you out of darkness into his marvellous light" (1 Pet. 2:9).

My friend, this should also tell you that you are different from all other people in the world. Being a child of God puts you in the line of royalty. When Peter talks about a royal priesthood, this is establishing a kingdom of priests. You see, God has a kingdom, and in that kingdom, His children must be of royal blood and are well trained in the affairs of the king's business. Take your position as a child of God.

Being filled with the Spirit of God is the key to being a son or daughter of God. The Scriptures tell us that the Spirit bears witness that we are His. Romans 8:16 says, "The Spirit itself beareth witness with our spirit, that we are the children of God."

The next characteristic that proves you are a child of God is the fact that you demonstrate God's love. When you have the Spirit of God, you will have love. My friend, this proves that you are a child of God. Jesus said that our love for one another would prove to the world that we are His disciples. John 13:35 says, "By this shall all men know that ye are my disciples, if ye have love one to another."

## WHAT PRIVILEGE YOU HAVE

The children of God now have access to the throne and presence of God. We also have access to the abundant blessings in Christ. Before Christ came to die on the cross, the priest went into the Most Holy Place of the temple and interceded before God on behalf of the people. On the cross, while Jesus cried out and gave up the ghost, the middle wall was torn down. This wall kept us on the outside of the temple and away from God.

Matthew 27:50–51 says, "Jesus, when he had cried again with a loud voice, yielded up the ghost. And, behold, the veil of the temple was rent in twain from the top to the bottom; and the earth did quake, and the rocks rent." At this moment on the cross, sin was finally dealt with and moved out of the way. **The partition wall that separated us from God was also torn down, allowing us to go into the Most Holy Place to talk with our Father on a one-on-one basis.** The priest no longer has the power of attorney to intercede on our behalf. We now have the power to go before God for ourselves.

## YOU HAVE A SON'S REWARD

Parents leave an inheritance for their children. A son is blessed with all the possessions of the parents. In the same way, all the blessings of the Lord belong to us.

Ephesians 1:11 says, "In whom also we have obtained an inheritance, being predestinated according to the purpose of him who worketh in all things after the counsel of his own will."

All the blessings of the kingdom of God are bestowed upon us as His children and not on those who are not His children. Ephesians 5:5 says, "For this ye know, that no whoremonger, nor unclean person, or covetous man, who is an idolater, hath any inheritance in the kingdom of Christ and of God."

You see, Christ died on the cross, and then the will of God came into effect. If the testator does not die, the will does not come into effect. **Christ died on the cross for us and thus effected the will of God in that He removed sin from us, brought us back into relationship with God, and released the eternal blessings of God into our lives.** Peace, joy, and happiness are also a part of the package that the child of God enjoys as one of His children.

## CHAPTER 5

# BE AN EXAMPLE

Children learn from example and what they see others do. A child sees an adult as his mentor and the best example to follow because the child tells himself that the adult knows the right way and the right things to do. The child places his trust in adults. That's why we ought to lead by example. Paul said, "Follow me as I follow Christ" (see 1 Corinthians 11:1). My friend, it is incumbent upon us to be very good examples in all things. This is in keeping with the spirit of the Bible, which intends to produce righteousness in all of us.

First Timothy 4:12 says, "Let no man despise thy youth; but be thou an example of the believers, in word, in conversation, in charity, in spirit, in faith, in purity." Although Timothy was a young person, this scripture is a good one that speaks to all concerning the spirit of righteousness that should be evident in our lives. Proverbs 14:34 says, "Righteousness exalts a nation, but sin is a reproach to any people."

Most times pastors preach messages that are directed at others, but for the message to be effective, it must first minister to him. **The pastor must first be obedient to the word himself and be convinced by it; then it will be most convincing to others so they can follow his example.** There is the saying "Do as I say, but not as I do." My friends, you must set an example with your life twenty-four hours a day. That's the greatest example anyone can be.

I know of a pastor who had an extramarital relationship with another woman. He was a very good preacher, and his church was doing well. The type of lifestyle he led was evident for all to see; those who claimed not to know were just turning a blind eye to the truth. Eventually the entire congregation started having similar types of relationships. Marriages started to break down, couples started to separate at a very fast pace, and before you knew it, the entire congregation was messed up with a lot of broken relationships.

Because of the position we hold and the office we occupy, it is of great importance for us to be good examples. The influence we have on people's lives could have far-reaching effects.

## WHAT YOU SHOULD BE DOING

When you work hard, your children will follow you as a role model for their lives. If they see that you are committed to family, dedicated to your job, and set yourself to solving problems that affect them and others, they may very well want to be just like you. They may also see that you are dedicated to prayer. You must have a balanced life. You can set the tone for your children to grow into loving and responsible people in society.

Galatians 6:7 says, "Be not deceived; God is not mocked: for whatsoever a man soweth, that shall he also reap." If you sow good into the lives of young people, you will get good out of them, but if you sow evil into their lives, you will get evil out of them. If you sow violence, that's exactly what you will get in return. It's natural for one to produce after its kind. So, we should be sowing seeds of righteousness in the lives of all whom we meet in life, both young and old alike.

## THE RIGHT ATMOSPHERE

My friend, you must place your young ones in the right environment and insulate them from bad influences. There is no perfect environment because all have their shortcomings. Very few children from terrible and violent backgrounds make it to a better life. A lot of them fall into gangs and other violent activity. The community in which we live does have a great measure of influence in the shaping of our character. However, a good thing can still come out of Nazareth.

## WE LEARN FROM WHAT WE SEE

It is just a few bad apples that spoil the whole basket. So we must narrow it down to the single-family home that will have the responsibility for raising its children according to the Bible.

I remember once at a service in our church during the time of giving, my first son, Joshua, was about three years old at the time. When the offering basket passed in front of him, he went into his mother's purse, took out her last two hundred dollars, and put it in the offering basket. At that moment, my wife was leading worship. After the service, it was told to her by another sister what Joshua had done.

Joshua did exactly what he saw us do every Sunday and on other occasions. He may not have known the amount to give, but he knew it was time to give when he saw the basket passing by. This is one example of children practicing the things they see adults do. That's why we should do good at all times, because we'll never know which child is looking at us.

## LOVE YOUR SPOUSE

Young men and women will also look at the way we treat our spouses. This is an area of our lives where we must be good examples. If we treat our wives badly with abuse and violence, then our sons will pattern the behavior we display and go on to be bad husbands and fathers themselves. The same applies to our female counterpart. Ephesians 5:25 says, "Husbands, love your wives, even as Christ also loved the church, and gave himself for it."

Husbands are compelled by Scripture to love their wives and make sacrifices for them. Give your wife a sense of security, and make her happy. Cherish your wife, and show affection to her; don't beat up on her. Sometimes it may mean forsaking your friends to maintain a good marriage relationship. Pray for your wife, and be the priest of the home. Others may desire to be just like you.

## LOVE YOUR NEIGHBOR

Loving yourself is very easy and effortless, but expressing love and extending it to others is a challenge. Jesus told the rich young ruler to go sell his possessions and distribute the gains of the sale to the poor. The ruler said this was a difficult thing. He refused to do what it takes to get eternal life. All he had to do was to obey the command of the master, Jesus Christ. This guy loved his possessions more than people and his own soul.

Matthew 19:21 says, "Jesus said unto him, If thou wilt be perfect, go and sell that thou hast, and give to the poor, and thou shalt have treasure in heaven: and come and follow me." Observe during the discourse from verses 16 to 21, the young ruler said that he had kept all this from his youth up. He didn't really love his neighbor, because Jesus was referring to the poor as his neighbor. Therefore, if he regarded the poor as his neighbor, he would have obeyed, sold what he had, and given to those who had need around him.

We need money to get by on a daily basis. We also need money for the work of the ministry of the kingdom of God. The message is not one that says it's not good to be rich, but rather it places God before riches and instructs us to show compassion to the poor, who are our real neighbors, to which Jesus referred.

## CHAPTER 6

# SITTING IDLY BY

Some parents make every effort to impart good values to their children and perhaps also to those children in the community in which they live. However, there are those parents who just don't have a sense of spiritual and moral values and don't care if Sunday falls on a Monday. *Qué será, sera,* "what is to be will be." My friend, such a way of life will do you no good. "Woe unto the man who knows the way and doeth it not" (Isa. 45:9).

## CHASTISING CAN BE HELPFUL

Some parents are familiar with a few scriptures and may have experienced the impartation of biblical text while attending Sunday school or church. Then there are those who are strong Christians but still allow their children to behave in an unmannerly way without restraint. When we know the right things, it is expected of us to do the right things. Remember, it is sin to know what you ought to do and then not do it (James 4:17).

**If you fail to chastise or discipline your children and let everything be just as it is, you leave room for negative development to take place in their lives.** Children need to be guided in the right direction. Procrastinating and sitting idly by are not part of the nature of the believer. When a child is left to himself, he could become lazy, complacent, and easily influenced. "Bad company corrupts good character" (1 Cor. 15:33).

My friend, I firmly believe that allowing a child to be on his own can contribute to spiritual and moral decay. Sitting it out will not help, but being vigilant in pursuit of righteousness will surely make great strides in the right direction. Righteousness and holiness, when manifested in our lives, can provoke others to righteousness. When you demonstrate a do-not-care attitude, quite a few lives that could have been saved might just go down the drain.

It takes only one person to make a difference. One person can change the course of history or change the world, for that matter. You may have the ability, the experience, and the training to help change the course of people's lives. But if you just sit by and allow them to go down to destruction, not only their own lives, but the lives of an entire generation could be affected negatively. Don't just sit it out and hope that one day things may get better, because that won't happen on its own. God has given you the ability to initiate change. You need to get up and do something.

## YOU HAVE THE POWER

My friend, God has given you the power to make things happen. He gave you the power to become rich; he gave you the power to speak life into situations and circumstances, according to Deuteronomy 8:18: "And you shall remember the LORD your God, for it is He who gives you power to get wealth that He may establish His covenant which He swore to your fathers, as it is this day." My friend, remember God when success comes your way. Also remember Luke 10:19: "Behold, I give unto you power to tread on serpents and scorpions and over all the power of the enemy: and nothing shall by any means hurt you."

God has given you the power to get wealth and the power over the abilities of the enemy of your soul. You possess the power to take control of your future and destiny. My friend, you have been given the ability to change your position in life. Speak life into your space as well as into other people's. Proverbs says that life and death are in the power of the tongue. **Be ambitious and not lazy, and generate wealth both for you, your family, and the work of the church of Jesus Christ.** Don't sit by and let the world around you fall apart, but be vigilant. You can be one of those people who watch things happen or one of those who wake up one morning and ask what happened. Or you can be one of those people who make things happen.

# CHAPTER 7

# THE CHURCH

## WHAT IS THE CHURCH?

The building you go to on Sundays to worship God is normally called the church. This term is used to describe a place of worship where the saints of God meet together in fellowship. However, the true sense of the word depicts a breathing, living entity. This is an organism that the Bible refers to as the body of Christ. In Matthew 16:18, the church is first mentioned: "And I say also unto thee, that thou art Peter, and upon this rock I will build my church; and the gates of hell shall not prevail against it."

In Matthew 16:13–19, there is a conversation between Jesus and His disciples. Peter answered the question that was asked, and Jesus said, "Thou art Peter and upon this rock I will build my church." This tells us that the church is built on a massive rock. Some folks think that Peter is the foundation of the church, but this is not so. *Peter* comes from the root word in Greek *petros*, meaning "a stone." A stone is not a rock. Jesus was referring to Himself as the rock when He said "upon this rock." Jesus used the word *petra* in the Greek, meaning "a massive rock." So Jesus is the foundation of the church. Paul also talks of Jesus as being the foundation in 1 Corinthians 3:11: "For other foundation can no man lay than that is laid, which is Jesus Christ." There is no other foundation for the church than Jesus Christ Himself, who is the rock on which the church is built.

## WHO IS THE CHURCH?

The word church is used of an assembly and in itself implies no more than a gathering of people who have been called forth. The word *church* is the Greek *ekklesia*, meaning "to call out." The word *ekklesia* also depicts a form of separation. This is the people of God called out of the world and separated for God's purpose. This is the body, or the gathering of people, who are called out from among all the people of the world and are set apart for the service of God.

Peter also talks of the church being called out of darkness into light. First Peter 2:9 says, "But ye are a chosen generation, a royal priesthood, an holy nation, a peculiar people; that ye should shew forth the praise of him who hath called you out of darkness into his marvellous light." **The world is seen as darkness, and therefore the church is called out of the dark world into being the light of God.**

In 1 Peter 2:5, the people of God are referred to as stones building the house, or the church of God: "Ye also, as lively stones, are built up a spiritual house, an holy priesthood, to offer up spiritual sacrifices, acceptable to God by Jesus Christ." This means that the people who are called out of the world are the lively stones that make up the building blocks of the church. Therefore, the church is the body of Christ; that is, the people who gather together, who are called from the unsaved world into the light of God. They are the true church of Jesus Christ.

## RELEVANCE OF THE CHURCH

This church started out in the power of God and the resurrected Christ, working miracles and healing the sick, the lame, and all manner of physical and spiritual sicknesses. In the book of Acts, you will see many accounts of the signs and wonders performed by members of the church. They were filled with the Holy

*The Church*

Spirit first. Acts 2:1–4 tells of the members of the church waiting in the upper room and then being filled with the Holy Ghost: "And they were all filled with the Holy Ghost, and began to speak with other tongues, as the Spirit gave them utterance" (v. 4).

You must be filled with the Spirit of God to be able to do miracles. Fear gripped the hearts of many, and they gave their lives to the Lord. The apostles did many other signs and wonders, causing others to be added to the church. Acts 2:47 says, "Praising God, and having favour with all the people. And the Lord added to the church daily such as should be saved." In Acts 3:1–11, Peter and John were going into the temple to pray and saw a lame man at the gate. The man was healed by looking on them. You see, they were filled with the Spirit of God and were also filled with faith.

Today it looks as if the church is not doing miracles like before. There are sick and demon-possessed people who are not being healed. Is it that there are not enough sick people? Or is it that the church has moved away from the preaching of faith? I think it is the latter, because the hospitals are overwhelmed and there are not sufficient beds. There are more sick people today than at any other time on earth.

The church is relevant for today. We need to get back to the preaching of faith. In James 5:15, we see that faith can save the sick: "And the prayer of faith shall save the sick, and the Lord shall raise him up; and if he hath committed sins, they shall be forgiven him."

We pray for people to be healed quite often and seldom see the desired results. This is because we pray without faith. Faith must be present in us for the power of God to heal and deliver folks from bondage. Jesus talks of the importance of faith for casting out devils in Matthew 17:20: "And Jesus said unto them, Because of your unbelief: for verily I say unto you, If you have faith as a grain of mustard seed, ye shall say unto this mountain, Remove hence to yonder place; and it shall remove: and nothing shall be impossible unto you."

The intent here is to drive the point home that faith is vital to the existence of the church. Clearly the church is lacking in faith. A mustard seed is the smallest of all seeds. If you have just a tiny speck of faith, you will do great things; you can cause a whole mountain to move from its position. A mountain is so large, yet a small amount of faith can move this giant structure. **A church full of faith in this modern time can change the course of this world and its condition.** We must get back to the place where we were and carry out the will and purposes of God. Jesus is coming soon for a church that is full of faith and free of impurities, a church that is living for Him, just like it started in the book of Acts.

The church deviated from the core message of the gospel to a more financial and appeasing one. You will notice that the messages coming from the pulpits of churches are no longer directed at the sinner to generate a spirit of repentance and conversion. **Oftentimes the pastors and preachers who stay the course are branded as traditionalists, preachers of doom and gloom, etc.** People who delve into sin and those who are not Christians should be motivated and convicted to change their lifestyles upon hearing a preacher's sermons. Instead, we have people not fearing for the condition of their soul and destiny because they are led to believe that it's okay to live any old how and not obey the truth of the gospel, once they contribute a huge sum of money to the welfare of the pastor and the church.

In some ways, pastors today encourage people to buy their salvation by way of the messages of prosperity and giving. For people to think that their salvation is secured because of the huge offerings they place in the hands of pastors is misleading and frivolous. These people continue to live sinful and adulterous lives because a loving pastor doesn't want to lose his offering.

I am not bashing prosperity—no, not for a moment. Neither am I against the rich. God desires His people to be wealthy. As Deuteronomy 8:18 says, **"You shall remember the Lord your God, for it is he who gives you power to get wealth, that he may confirm his covenant that he swore to your fathers, as it is this day."** Paul also says that he prays that we prosper: "Beloved, I wish above all things that thou mayest prosper and be in health, even as thy soul prospereth" (3 John 2). So this issue is not being against blessings and prosperity. This issue is one where the message of the gospel has been shifted from the Great Commission to one that neglects the preaching of salvation and stresses the preaching of materialism.

## GET BACK ON COURSE

My friends, these are indeed the last days, or the end times, as some will prefer to say. Tithes and offerings are there to help the widows and those who are unable to work for some reason or the other. If you obey the Scriptures, some of the critics that the church attracts will be minimized.

First of all, you need to take a time-out. Step down from the pulpit for a period of time, seeking God for direction in fasting and praying. You must seek repentance and God's forgiveness for the wrongs that were done. You must humble yourself under the mighty hand of God. "Unless you are converted and become like children, you will not enter the kingdom of heaven. **Whoever then humbles himself as this child, he is the greatest in the kingdom of heaven**" (Matt. 18:3–4).

You will be brought low if you refuse to humble yourself. It may be just a matter of time before you fall. When pastors are filled with pride and refuse to manifest humility, they fall hard. This means that the ministries they've worked so hard to build come crashing down, and their spiritual lives spiral downward.

Humility is vital to the success of any man of God. Moses was used by God to perform many miracles, yet he was humble. God said that Moses was the meekest among men: "Now the man Moses was very meek, above all the men who were upon the face of the earth" (Num. 12:3). Meekness and humility are the cure for pride and arrogance.

Jesus was God in the flesh, yet He humbled Himself. Matthew 11:29–30 says, "Take my yoke upon you, and learn of me; for I am meek and lowly in heart: and ye shall find rest unto your souls. For my yoke is easy, and my burden is light." Jesus and Moses were the two mightiest men to walk the earth, and they left a legacy of humility and meekness for all to follow. Friends, we must do the same in order to carry out our mandate for the church of Jesus Christ.

You must set the administration of the church in the right perspective after seeking God's face for guidance. All the lay ministers and officers of the church must also follow the examples of Christ and the man Moses. We all together must stop hoarding the wealth of the church and start distributing it to those who are in real need. It's time we start executing the business of the church of God.

## THE BRIDE OF CHRIST

When Jesus comes again, He is coming for His bride. The church is also called the bride of Christ. Revelation 19:7 stresses the readiness of the bride: "Let us be glad and rejoice, and give honour to him: for the marriage of the Lamb is come, and his wife hath made herself ready." This is sometimes

*The Church*

referred to as the marriage supper of the Lamb. This is the consummation of the marriage of Christ and the church as His bride. This is in keeping with the Middle Eastern pattern of marriage in those days, covering three stages:

1. The betrothal, which was legally binding, occurs when the individual members of the body of Christ are saved.
2. The coming of the Bridegroom for His bride occurs at the rapture of the church.
3. The marriage supper of the Lamb occurs in connection with the second coming of Christ.

This was the custom of marriages in those days.

Those who are saved are part of the church, and they belong to Christ because the church is His bride. The bridegroom comes and takes the bride from her parents' house.

Jesus is the Bridegroom, and the church is His bride, and He is coming again to receive her unto Himself. She must be ready. To be ready, the church must be preaching faith, be full of His Spirit, and be doing His will, just as the early church did. The present church and the early church are one and the same.

A bride sets herself apart for her groom. The church must prepare herself for the return of the Bridegroom, Jesus Christ. It is imperative that you, my friend, be ready for the coming of the Lord, and He must find you doing the things that you should be doing. You should be sharing the love of God, worshiping and praising Him in all things, and at the same time seeking to save souls from hell's damnation.

# CHAPTER 8

# WHAT GOD WANTS

## PRIDE AND DESTRUCTION

It is not God's intention to have a messed-up world. It was never His intention for the world to be lost because of godlessness and sin. **In fact, God created the heavens and the earth perfect.** Genesis 1:1 says, "In the beginning God created the heavens and the earth." This means that everything was already created—the trees, the animals, fishes, and all life—and was perfect until Genesis 1, verse 2.

Genesis 1:2 reads, "And the earth was without form, and void; and darkness was upon the face of the deep. And the Spirit of God moved upon the face of the waters." Something took place between verse 1 and verse 2 to cause the earth to be without form and void. One idiot, a created being called Satan, or Lucifer, decided to try to get God's creation to bow down and worship him instead of God. God revealed the scenario to Isaiah.

Isaiah 14:12–14 says, "How art thou fallen from heaven, O Lucifer, son of the morning! How art thou cut down to the ground, which didst weaken the nations! For thou hast said in thine heart, **I will ascend into heaven, I will exalt my throne above the stars of God: I will sit also upon the mount of the congregation, in the sides of the north:** I will ascend above the heights of the clouds; I will be like the most High." Satan and one-third of the angels were cast out of heaven and onto the earth, causing chaos and destruction. He was cast out because of the pride that filled his heart.

## GET PRIDE OUT OF YOUR HEART!

My friend, pride leads to destruction. Proverbs 16:18 states, **"Pride goeth before** destruction, and an haughty spirit **before** a fall." Pride keeps people trapped in a prison called "self." There are only three persons in that prison: **me, myself, and I.** It is a very lonely place. Pride hinders God from reaching and using people who are filled with such a destructive character trait.

A person filled with pride shows disrespect to others, and he will be stingy and always demanding to be first and to be at the top of everything. Pride wants to be seen, noticed, pampered, and made comfortable and excited. Pride destroyed Lucifer, making him the king of selfishness; he is powerfully self-righteous. Pride makes you think about yourself, and it makes you become inconsiderate. Get pride out of your life!

**Be a prisoner of humility. Humility is**

**satisfying, knowing that God is in control. It trusts, and it enjoys rest and peace. It is obedient and joyful and delights in making others happy.** You could never have pride and be successful, for pride kills success!

## FELLOWSHIP WITH GOD

My friend, since the fall of man in the Garden of Eden, sin and evil entered this world. From generation to generation, sin has raised its ugly head, causing pain and misery in the lives of people everywhere. However, what God wants is for us to be free from the pain of sin and evil of this world. That's why His Son Jesus Christ came to earth to die: so we could be rejoined to God and have fellowship with Him.

Romans 5:8 says, "But God commendeth his love toward us, in that, while we were yet sinners, Christ died for us." Though sin separates us eternally from God, God Himself wants us to be reconciled to Him by our recognizing that we must repent of sin and believe on Jesus so we can be free from sin.

Romans 6:23 reads, "For the wages of sin is death; but the gift of God is eternal life through Jesus Christ our Lord." God's desire is for you to enjoy eternal life, walk victoriously in His blessings, and fellowship with Him. No matter what challenges you face, God is with you.

## OBEDIENCE IS IMPORTANT

My friend, God also desires you to be obedient to Him and His Word. My grandmother always said, "Obedience is heaven's first law." If Adam had not sinned and disobeyed God in the Garden of Eden, the world might not be in the condition it is in today. God sees from beginning to ending, and obeying Him will save a lifetime of pain.

Deuteronomy 6:2–3 says, "That thou mightest fear the Lord thy God, to keep all his statutes and his commandments, which

I command thee, thou, and thy son, and thy son's son, all the days of thy life, and that thy days may be prolonged. Hear therefore, O Israel, and observe to do it, that it may be well with thee, and that ye may increase mightily, as the Lord God of thy fathers hath promised thee, in the land that floweth with milk and honey." The message of these two verses is clear: wherever you go, always obey God. Once you obey God, don't mind the type of influence in the nation, country, community, work, or school; He will protect you and bless you.

The term *milk and honey* refers to the provisions made by our heavenly Father. In the midst of famine, we will have plenty to go around. Because we teach our children to obey God, we will do well. David puts it nicely in Psalm 23:6: "Surely goodness and mercy shall follow me all the days of my life; and I will dwell in the house of the Lord forever." That's the desire God wants for us: to enjoy eternal blessings and have His goodness and mercy follow us wherever the soles of our feet touch.

# CHAPTER 9

# HOW CAN WE RETURN?

Most churches in the world have moved away from the fundamental principles and foundation of Christ. Church attendance from the late twentieth century to the twenty-first century has fallen drastically. In England during the 1970s, 80 percent of the people were Christians and attended church regularly on a Sunday and during the week as well. In 2007, that number had changed significantly, with less than 44 percent attending church.

**This drop in church attendance shows one of two things:**

1. The importance of attending church has not been passed on from parent to child.
2. People no longer have faith in the church's systems.

Most people have lost faith for some reason or the other. Luke 18:8 says, "I tell you that he will avenge them speedily. Nevertheless, when the son of man cometh, will he find faith on the earth?" Jesus asked that question, knowing that many would fall away from the faith. In the following verse of that same chapter, He talked about those who trust in themselves instead of the righteousness of God. That's where we are today. Also, the apostle Paul warned Timothy of what would occur in the last days: "Now the Spirit speaketh expressly, that in the latter times some shall depart from the faith, giving heed to seducing spirits, and doctrines of devils" (1 Tim. 4:1).

These verses express that there is a lack of faith and that there will be a great falling away. You see, people have substituted entertainment and other forms of social events for church services and spirituality. Not that entertainment and socializing are not good—they do have their place. But when they replace faith and righteousness, going to church just becomes a formality. Getting back to the place where we used to be is then very difficult. We must recognize the need for drastic action in the spiritual realm and in the physical realm as well. **This situation is drastic, and therefore the fight to reclaim our position and relevance in society must be drastic.** Drastic circumstances calls for drastic measures.

## BE GENUINE

To return, we must get back to fundamental Christian principles that were neglected in practice for a period of time or if practiced at all were in the minority. Prayer must be first on the agenda, followed by the study of the Word of God. Bible study and prayer meetings today have become a formality. **We need to be sincere with ourselves and return to the place of sincere prayer and studying of the Word of God and unearth deep spiritual truths from the Word.** We must also express these truths without fear or favor.

Second Timothy 2:15 reads, "Study to shew thyself approved unto God, a workman that needeth not to be ashamed, rightly dividing the word of truth." You will not misinterpret the Word if you rightly divide it, and you will not be put to shame when you have correct knowledge. James 5:16 shows that sincere prayer works: "The effectual fervent prayer of a righteous man availeth much." This means intense spiritual prayer effectually producing the desired results. It's not just a form of godliness, but real genuine prayer with knowledge and faith.

## BE RIGHTEOUS

We must return to righteousness, which is an integral part of our position as the church. No wonder Proverbs 14:34 says, "Righteousness exalts a nation: but sin is a reproach to any people." Abraham's faith was counted to him for righteousness: "And he believed in the Lord; and he counted it to him for righteousness" (Gen. 15:6).

Believing God and obeying His Word could be counted to you for righteousness. You may not know what the outcome of something may be, but you believe that God will work it out, so you obey Him. Believing **God is blindly doing exactly what He asks you to do even though you can't see the next moment or the future.**

Faith can accomplish anything we purpose to do. There is no stopping the church when we express our faith in Christ, for faith is the victory that overcomes the world. A fundamental part of our character is faith in Jesus Christ's resurrection. In 1 Corinthians 15:13, the Bible says, "But if there be no resurrection of the dead, then is Christ not risen." Expressing faith in Christ is tantamount to our returning to that place.

## LEARN TO ADAPT

For the lukewarm and the unsaved, we must bridge the gap with the tools we have available to us. By this I mean use social networking systems like Twitter, Facebook, and others. Plan social events with a gospel tone to get the message across. For younger people who love the outdoors, organize hikes and other sporting activities. Jesus and His disciples used the tools available to them during their time on earth. We can do the same. Technology will change and progress, but the gospel will remain the same.

Christianity is not boring, as some say it is. We can have fun while we maintain our holiness.

**We can return to our foundation using every available avenue without compromising holiness and salvation.** However, returning to where we used to be will take people who have a passion and burden for souls and who also have the spirit of boldness. Returning to our first love also means that we will have to sacrifice other activities to devote time to see changes happen. This will take a lot of time because some changes don't occur overnight. It may take a long time to yield the desired results.

Romans 5:4 says, "And patience, experience; and experience, hope." Patience is another characteristic we must have for the long journey back to that place. Believe me when I say that you will need patience. You will be ridiculed, bombarded with accusations of all kinds, and made fun of because of your righteousness. Prepare yourself for it as you start your journey back to the place where you used to be.

# CHAPTER 10

# VICTORY IS AROUND THE CORNER

God promises a prize for those who run the race to the end. Many start the race with enthusiasm and vigor but lose steam and interest for some reason or the other. First Corinthians 9:24 reminds us, "Know ye not that they which run in a race run all, but one receiveth the prize? So run that ye may obtain." There is a prize for those who run well in this race. It is not about the one who runs the fastest, but the one who finishes the race. **The race is not for the swift, but it's for the one who runs with patience and perseverance.**

Hebrews 12:1 says, "Wherefore, seeing we also are compassed about with so great a cloud of witnesses, let us lay aside every weight, and the sin which doth so easily beset us, and let us run with patience the race that is set before us." Patience is a main ingredient in winning the prize. Indeed a lot of mighty men around us are falling, and some are dropping out of the race. This is disheartening and very discouraging for Christians who are concerned about the position of the church. You may feel like you are all alone, but you are not. You have the most important person by your side, Jesus. This is what He said in Matthew 28:20: **"And, lo, I am with you always, even unto the end of the world."** So remember, you are not alone!

## COMING UNDER ATTACK

Second Corinthians 4:8 tells us that we are bombarded on every side, hard pressed, etc., but in the end, if we keep faith in the midst of adversity, we will be victorious. God is saying that He will deliver us when we go through trials.

Your trials will not overcome you. You will walk out victoriously on the other side. Isaiah 43:2 says, "When thou passest through the waters, I will be with thee; and through the rivers, they will not overflow thee: when thou walkest through the fire, thou shalt not be burned; neither shall the flame be kindled upon thee."

In this verse, **God promises that the fire will not burn you, and the floodwaters will not drown you or carry you away**. This represents the pressures of life that frustrate you and also make you feel as if nothing is working out for you no matter how hard you try. You see, these attacks and bombardments come to break your will. The aim of the devil is to do just that and cause you to bow to him and not obey God and His Word. In Luke 4:1–13, the devil pressured, bombarded, and tempted the Lord. Based on the Word of God expressed openly, the devil himself gave up and left. Take God at His word and you will see how He will work things out for His faithful.

## ENDURE TO THE END

In order to attain victory in this battle for life, you must endure hardness as a good soldier. Soldiers are trained to endure and withstand pressure. Both mental and physical stress might break the ordinary man, but a soldier who is well trained and disciplined will outlast the pressure and attacks. As 2 Timothy 2:3–4 says, "Thou therefore endure hardness as a good soldier of Jesus Christ. No man that warreth entangleth himself with the affairs of this life, that he may please him who hath chosen him to be a soldier."

Good soldiers fight to the end. Even when their strength begins to fail, they still hold on to hope. As Isaiah 40:31 says, "But they that wait upon the Lord shall renew their strength; they shall mount up with wings as eagles; they shall run, and not be weary; and they shall walk, and not faint." **As you endure, your strength will fail; however, the Lord will renew your strength, just like the eagles'**. The eagle is the longest-living bird; he outlives all the other birds. When the eagle ages, his feathers begin to fall off, and what remains on him becomes soggy and sticks together, making the bird unable to fly. This happens when the eagle becomes weary. Also, the eyes become dim because scales form on the eyelids.

The eagle finds himself by the brook of running water. He soaks his head in the water and knocks the scales on his eyelids onto a rock until the scales fall off. The eagle will soak his body in the water then pluck out his feathers one by one until he is naked. This process renews his strength. Fresh feathers grow out, and the eyes become bright again. In other words, his strength has been restored and his youth renewed, enabling him to soar high just like before. In this same way, your strength can be restored so that you can endure the battle to the end. God will always give you the strength you need to carry on.

## YOU WILL BE DELIVERED

Three young men—Shadrach, Meshach, and Abednego—captives from Israel taken to Babylon, were placed in a furnace seven times hotter than normal. This happened because they refused to bow to the king's image. Daniel 3:16–28 paints a picture of what took place.

**Before being placed in the fire, the three men stood their ground by not bowing to the demands of the king that violated their fundamental beliefs.** Inside the fire, they were saved by the Son of God. These three guys could have easily given up, but they chose not to do so. These guys manifested their faith in the Son of the living God, who visited them inside the fire. God delivered them from the king, at the same time bringing glory to Himself, proving that He is the God who answers the prayers of His people.

## KNOW YOUR ENEMY

Peter tells us that our enemy the devil walks about seeking whom he may devour: "Be sober, be vigilant; because your adversary the devil, as a roaring lion, walketh about, seeking whom he may devour" (1 Pet. 5:8).

Take note of the strategies of the devil, and look at the deceptive ways he possesses. He is the father of lies, because he was a liar from the beginning. Lies are what he uses to deceive people. In the Garden of Eden, he twisted God's words and deceived Eve. Deception is the character of the enemy. You are being watched by the enemy, so you need to watch him.

Paul encourages us to give no place to the devil. He can use against us hate, unforgiveness, and an idle tongue, but 1 Timothy 5:14 says, "Give none occasion to the adversary to speak reproachfully." **In other words, we must watch our conversation, and we should always forgive others for the wrongs they commit against us.** Jesus said to forgive seventy times seven.

Second Corinthians 2:10–11 reads, "To whom ye forgive anything, I forgive also: for if I forgave anything, to whom I forgave it, for your sakes forgave I it in the person of Christ; lest Satan should get an advantage over us: for we are not ignorant concerning his devices." Forgiveness is a vital part of Christian character. Staying free of all offenders and releasing them from our hearts will give the devil no place to hold us in his vise.

## THE PRICE WAS PAID

Jesus already paid the price for our victory. Colossians 2:15 says it clearly: "And having spoiled principalities and powers, he made a shew of them openly, triumphing over them in it." **When Jesus died on the cross, He bruised the head of the serpent, that old devil, and bought back our freedom.** The Lord dealt a blow to the enemy that he cannot recover from up to this day. Jesus triumphed over the enemy of our souls; therefore, we are victors because we are joint heirs with Christ.

Romans 8:37 proclaims, "Nay, in all these things we are more than conquerors through him that loved us." A conqueror is one who overcomes his enemy, and Christ has overcome the enemy of our souls. We are more than conquerors because Christ has given to us the victory over the enemy. This means that without firing one shot at the enemy, you have the victory.

"Behold, I give unto you power to tread on serpents and scorpions, and over all the power of the enemy: and nothing shall by any means hurt you" (Luke 9:19). When your enemy the devil looks at you, he sees the authority of the power of Christ upon you. **He realizes that you know who you are and that you have the victory over him and all his demons.** You must continue to express your victory at all times. A dear price was paid so that you could enjoy it.

# About The Author

For the past twelve years, Lex Francois has been sharing the Word of God with many people. He was born on the island of Trinidad and Tobago, West Indies. Lex had an encounter with the Lord in 1992 that changed his life from that point onward. He attended the Bible Way Institute in 1995, where he graduated with a diploma in comprehensive Bible studies.

In 2004, he became the assistant director of Slow Gospel Music Ministries, a ministry that does distribution of food and clothing to the less fortunate, inclusive of prayer and intercession. He is also an announcer on the program *Slow Gospel Music* on two radio frequencies: Isaac 98.1 FM and Inspirational Radio 730 AM.

Lex is married to Alicia, and together they have two children, Joshua and Josiah. He is also the messenger of the book called *The Way We Were*.

# Acknowledgments

I must say thanks to God the Father of our Lord and Savior Jesus Christ for the inspiration and knowledge to put this powerful book together.

And to my friend, Mr. Nicholas C. Charles, I sincerely express my gratitude to you for your hard work and dedication to the success of this book. Mr. Charles played a vital part in putting this book together. He is also the author of many books, and you can look for those bearing his name.

I must also show recognition to Angelina James, (my mother)…and Monica Patrick for their contributions to my life as a child, and also heartfelt thanks to Dr. Kenny Mohansingh, the founder of Bible Way Institute, for impartation of knowledge in my life.

Last but not least, to my wife Alicia for her continued prayers and support. She is really a wonderful woman.

# Bibliography

All Scripture quotes are from the King James Version of the Bible. Copyright 1989 by World Publishing, Nashville, TN. Printed in the United States of America.

Also, some additional information from Campus Crusade for Christ, Trinidad and Tobago.

www.ingramcontent.com/pod-product-compliance
Ingram Content Group UK Ltd.
Pitfield, Milton Keynes, MK11 3LW, UK
UKHW041944230426
12048UKWH00008B/132